the little
b
of

CW00920556

E'S SHOP

Written and edited by Gill Knappett.
The author has asserted her moral rights.
Designed by Tim Noel-Johnson.
All photographs © Jarrold Publishing, except:
pp26–27 and 34 by kind permission of
The Oxford Story; p70 by kind permission of
Queen's Lane Coffee House.
The quote on p16 (Dorothy L. Sayers, *Gaudy Night*)
is reproduced by kind permission of
New English Library.

Printed in Hong Kong.
ISBN 0-7117-2434-2   1/03

Jarrold Publishing, Healey House, Dene Road, Andover,
Hampshire, SP10 2AA.
Tel: 01264 409200   e-mail: heritagesales@jarrold.com
website: www.britguides.com

Introduction

What is Oxford? An enigmatic mix of young and old, of town and gown, of celebrated culture and 21st-century entertainment, of energetic changes and centuries-old traditions … it is all these things, and more. *The Little Book of Oxford* will tempt, tease and tantalize with over 100 intriguing nuggets of information about this vibrant, multi-cultural city – some to make you think, some to make you smile, but all special reminders of this timeless place.

The finest city

This Oxford, I have no doubt,
is the finest City in the world …

John Keats

Compact fact

Oxford's impressive collection of
buildings is contained within
a space less than 1.6 square kilometres
(1 square mile).

Cleverly camouflaged

In 1142 the Empress Matilda was held
captive at Oxford Castle by King Stephen.
She escaped across the ice-covered river
during a snowstorm, camouflaged in a
white sheet.

Historic remains

All that remains of Oxford Castle is The Mound and St George's Tower, the walls of which are 2.7 metres (9ft) thick at the base.

High spots

The four best viewpoints from which to admire the city's spectacular skyline are Carfax Tower, The Tower of St Michael at the North Gate, the tower of the University Church of St Mary the Virgin and the Sheldonian Theatre's cupola.

Dreaming spires

And that sweet city with her dreaming spires,
She needs not June for beauty's heightening,
Lovely all times she lies, lovely to-night!

Matthew Arnold, 'Thyrsis', 1866

The smallest and the largest

Christ Church cathedral is the smallest cathedral in England and yet it serves the largest diocese.

Tom's timekeeping

Services at Christ Church take place in 'Cathedral Time', that kept by Tom Tower, which is five minutes behind Greenwich Mean Time.

Wizard inspiration

Christ Church's Great Hall and grand
staircase were the inspiration for
Hogwarts School in the film *Harry Potter
and the Sorcerer's Stone*.

Oxford's oldest

The 11th-century tower of the Church of St Michael at the North Gate is Oxford's oldest building and formed part of the city wall defences.

English Pope

The only Englishman to be elected Pope is Nicolas Breakspear, Vicar of Binsey – a hamlet near Oxford – in the early 12th century.

Oxford Martyrs

The Martyr's Memorial in St Giles honours the Oxford Martyrs – Protestant leaders Archbishop Cranmer, Bishop Ridley and Bishop Latimer – who were imprisoned in Bocardo prison by the Catholic Queen Mary I, cross-examined

in the Divinity School and tried for heresy in St Mary's Church. In October 1555 Cranmer was forced to watch from St Michael's tower as Ridley and Latimer were burned at the stake.

Cranmer met the same fate a few months later, even though he had renounced his faith in writing several times; once again reaffirming his Protestant beliefs, he first thrust his right hand, which had signed the recantations, into the flames.

Radcliffe I

The word 'camera' – as in Radcliffe Camera – means 'chamber'. This structure was financed by Dr John Radcliffe, an 18th-century physician, to house a library devoted to the sciences. Designed by James Gibbs, it was the first round library in the world and is now a private reading room for the Bodleian Library.

Radcliffe II

'... in Radcliffe Square the Camera slept like a cat in the sunshine, disturbed only by the occasional visit of a slow-footed don ...'.

Dorothy L. Sayers, *Gaudy Night*, 1935

Bodleian books

A copy of every book published in the United Kingdom is held in the Bodleian Library, an arrangement dating back to 1610. None of the books is allowed to leave the premises and new shelving stretching to 2.4 kilometres (1 1/2 miles) is required each year.

Ghostly happenings I

The ghost of Thomas Bodley, who founded the Bodleian Library, haunts the library of Merton College where he studied Greek and Hebrew.

Sheldonian sculptures

The Sheldonian Theatre, opened in 1669, was Christopher Wren's first large-scale masterpiece. The 13 sculpted heads adorning the railings are commonly referred to as 'Emperors' or 'Caesars' and

were commissioned by Wren to mirror the boundary stones in Rome which were often decorated with carved heads. Created by William Byrd, they have been replaced twice, in the 1860s and 1970s.

Encaenia

Each June the Sheldonian Theatre hosts Encaenia, a ceremony commemorating the university founders at which honorary degrees are bestowed on famous people from all over the world.

Europe's oldest

The Holywell Music Room, which opened in 1748 with a performance of Handel's 'Esther', claims to be the oldest surviving concert hall in Europe.

Poetic licence

At the Holywell Music Room in the 1920s, one Thomas Driberg recited his poems through a megaphone to an accompaniment of typewriters. The performance ended with the loud flushing of the lavatory, in those days situated just behind the platform!

Annual festival

Handel spent a week in Oxford in 1733, heralding the debut performance of his oratorio *Athalia*. His visit is commemorated with an annual festival.

Oxford Symphony

In the late 18th century Haydn received an honorary Doctorate of Music at Oxford; his Symphony No. 92 was played during his visit and is known as the Oxford Symphony.

Tradescant's travels

The Ashmolean Museum's collection of art and antiquities is based on the artefacts acquired in the 17th century by royal

gardener John Tradescant who travelled Europe in search of rare plants. A cup on display in the museum was, until recently, said to be made from a unicorn's horn; sadly, it is now known to be rhinoceros.

Dead as a dodo

The remains of Europe's last dodo – now extinct – are displayed in the University Museum of Natural History.

The dodo and the knight

The Dodo in *Alice's Adventures in Wonderland* and the White Knight in *Through the Looking-Glass* are said to represent the books' author, Lewis Carroll, who was educated at Oxford.

The Oxford Story

Visitors to The Oxford Story are taken on a 30-minute ride sitting at old-fashioned school desks, enjoying sights and sounds – and even smells – of scenes from the city's history.

E = mc²

Einstein's blackboard
is housed in the
Museum of the
History of Science
in Broad Street.

It won't hurt a bit

The first intravenous
injection of penicillin
was given to a patient
at the Radcliffe
Infirmary in 1941.

Blenheim Palace

In 1704 Queen Anne presented the Duke of Marlborough, John Churchill, with the land that is now the Blenheim Palace estate – situated

13 kilometres (8 miles) outside Oxford – in recognition of his victory at the Battle of Blenheim.

Marlborough Maze

At 0.4 hectares (over an acre) the Marlborough Maze at Blenheim Palace is the world's largest symbolic hedge maze.

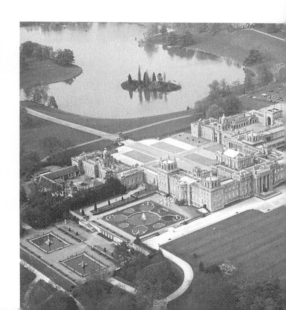

Winston's wit

Sir Winston Churchill was asked whether his mother was at a ball in the Long Library or out with a shooting party in the park just before his birth at Blenheim Palace. He responded, 'Although present on that occasion, I have no clear recollection of the events leading up to it.'

Where's the university?

Oxford University consists of over 30 colleges dotted around the city, each a community in its own right – there is not one central campus.

University beginnings

In the 12th century a university evolved in the market town of Oxford when scholars and tutors, forbidden to study at the University of Paris by Henry II, settled here. For many years most students were educated for a career in the Church; the dominance of religion at Oxford continued until the early 20th century.

Town v. Gown

As the university grew and gained in strength and wealth during the 14th century, the townspeople's resentment resulted in regular fights between town and gown. The university would summon its forces by ringing the bells of St Mary's, while the town would rally to the peal of bells from St Martin's at Carfax. The scholars – backed by the monarch and the Church – were invariably the victors.

St Scholastica's Day Riot

The infamous St Scholastica's Day Riot of 1355 – depicted here in a scene from The Oxford Story – was caused by the discontent between town and gown, culminating in a pot of wine being hurled at the innkeeper of Swyndlestock Tavern at Carfax by a student. A three-day battle ensued in which over 60 students were killed and many more injured.

Honouring St Mary

Magdalen College honours St Mary Magdalen, although curiously its name has always been pronounced 'maudlin'.

Invocation to spring

Spring is heralded with an invocation sung in Latin by the Magdalen College School Choir from the college's Gothic bell tower at 6 o'clock each May Day morning.

May Morning mayhem

Magdalen's May Morning celebration is attended by an appreciative audience of thousands who gather at Magdalen Bridge, although at one time the choristers would pelt the crowd with rotten eggs, and the onlookers in turn would blow horns to drown out the singing.

Reluctant chorister

A choirmaster is said to have once brought a reluctant boy with a beautiful voice in chains from the country to sing in Magdalen's choir.

Ugly mugs

Amongst the gargoyles at Magdalen are carvings of wrestlers, a jester, a greyhound, a werewolf and a camel with an animal on its back.

House of Christ

Christ Church – never called Christ Church College – is traditionally referred to as 'The House' after its Latin name *Aedes Christi* (House of Christ).

Must be a record

In a period spanning 200 years, starting in 1762, Christ Church produced 16 British Prime Ministers.

Sneaky snipper

Ralph Kettell, at one time President of Trinity College, hid scissors in a muff and cut off the locks of long-haired students.

Ghostly happenings II

At St John's College the ghost of
Archbishop William Laud, President of the
college in 1611 and executed in 1645 for
treason, is said to bowl his head along the
ground to land at the feet of anyone
unfortunate enough to see the apparition.

A boarish tale

The Boar's Head ceremony, which takes place each Christmas at The Queen's College, commemorates a medieval scholar who, when studying the collected works of Aristotle on Shotover Hill, defended himself from an attacking wild boar by stuffing the book down its throat.

First quad
New College was the first to be designed around a quadrangle, which all of Oxford's colleges now have.

Keep off the grass
Visitors to Oxford's colleges must not walk on the grass – this privilege is reserved only for senior members of each college.

Weather report
Merton College kept Europe's first weather records in the 14th century.

Oldest library

Merton College's Mob Quad has the oldest library in England still in use, dating from 1378. It contains an astrolabe thought to have been used by Geoffrey Chaucer more than 600 years ago.

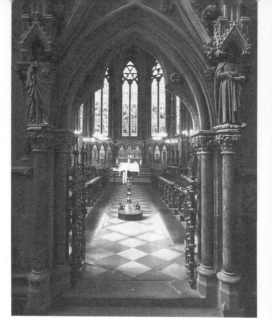

Two great artists

A tapestry in Exeter College's chapel depicting the Adoration of the Magi was designed by Edward Burne-Jones and made by William Morris; the two great artists met here as undergraduates in 1853.

Casson's comment

'If you like this sort of thing, this is the sort of thing you will like.'

Sir Hugh Casson commenting on Exeter College's chapel, the design of which is a subject of mixed opinion

Morse's last moment

Inspector Morse collapsed outside the chapel on Exeter College's quad in the final televised episode, *The Remorseful Day*.

TIC tours

Inspector Morse Walking Tours, starting from the Tourist Information Centre, follow in the footsteps of Oxford's most famous television detective.

Film set
Oriel Square, with its 18th-century houses, is one of Oxford's most filmed places.

Waugh memorial
Evelyn Waugh used his experiences as an undergraduate at Hertford College when writing *Brideshead Revisited*.

Bridge of Sighs

The Bridge of Sighs, named after its Venetian counterpart, links the north and south sites of Hertford College.

Knit one, purl one

Keble College has various nicknames, including the 'Knitted College' and 'Fair Isle Jersey' because of its unusual patterned edifice of red, black and cream-coloured brickwork.

Rights for women

Women were first accepted at Oxford in 1878 but did not sit the university's examinations until 1894 and were not awarded degrees until 1920.

Women only

St Hilda's is the only remaining all-female college – the others are now mixed.

No women allowed

Until the 1960s an undergraduate could be sent down if a woman was found in his rooms after midnight.

Tip-top tap trophy

It was reputed that if a man managed to have a bath in a women's college, he was allowed to wear a navy blue tie

emblazoned with silver taps. If he was able to produce the actual bath taps, he was entitled to gold taps on the tie.

Wilde I

Oscar Wilde, who came to Oxford in 1874, was a brilliant if eccentric student who took his pet lobster for walks. He recalled his time at Oxford as 'the most flower-like time of one's life'.

Wilde II

'Untruthful! My nephew Algernon? Impossible! He is an Oxonian.'

Lady Bracknell in Oscar Wilde's
The Importance of Being Earnest, 1895

Unpaid fine

In 1728 Samuel Johnson – a student at Pembroke College – was fined tuppence for missing a lecture; he refused to pay, saying it wasn't worth a penny.

Spoonerisms

The Reverend W. A. Spooner (1844–1930) enjoyed a 60-year association with Oxford University. A scholar at New College, he went on to lecture in history, philosophy and divinity, later serving as dean, warden and president. Famous for his Spoonerisms – his habit of transposing the first letters of one or more words – he reprimanded one student with 'you have hissed my mystery lecture', adding 'you have tasted two worms'.

TO THE MEMORY OF
PERCY BYSSHE SHELLEY.
POET.
BORN AT FIELD PLACE IN THE COUNTY OF SUSSEX, AUGUST 4, 1792.
DROWNED BY THE UPSETTING OF HIS BOAT IN THE GULF OF SPEZIA, JULY, 1822.
HIS ASHES ARE INTERRED IN THE PROTESTANT BURIAL GROUND AT ROME.

Wayward student

The most famous undergraduate to be
sent down was the poet Shelley in 1811.
He behaved appallingly during his six
months at University College but the final
straw was his production of a pamphlet
entitled 'The Necessity of Atheism'.

Believe it or not

Benjamin Jowett, a Master of Balliol College in the 19th century, warned an atheist student that he would be sent down if he did not believe in God by the next morning.

For Betjeman's benefit

John Betjeman (1906–84) chose to study medieval Welsh at Oxford, knowing full well that there was no one there to teach it, which meant a tutor travelled from Wales each week just for his benefit. He left university without a degree.

Another first

Margaret Thatcher, an undergraduate in the 1940s, was appointed as the first female president of the Oxford University Conservative Association.

Liddell inspiration

Alice Liddell, the inspiration for Lewis Carroll's Alice in *Alice's Adventures in Wonderland*, was the daughter of the Dean of Christ Church.

Pen name

Charles Dodgson lived at Christ Church for 47 years, first as an undergraduate and then as a maths don. It was when he wrote for a student paper that he was given the pseudonym Lewis Carroll, a name based on a reversed and Latinised version of his first two names, Charles Lutwidge.

Inklings' drinking place

The Eagle and Child pub, known locally as
The Bird and Baby, was the meeting place
of the Inklings, a group of academic and
literary men which included C.S. Lewis
and J.R.R. Tolkien.

Shakespeare's stopover

William Shakespeare often stayed at No. 3 Cornmarket Street to break his journey from Stratford to London. Visitors can view his room by appointment with its current occupants, the 'Oxford Aunts' — a nursing agency.

Super groups

Successful Oxford trio Supergrass are perhaps best known for their hit 'Alright' which reached No. I in the charts during the summer of 1995. And the five members of another famous group — the rock band Radiohead — met as schoolboys in Abingdon.

Oxford University Press

The Oxford University Press was started in the 16th century to print ancient manuscripts. In the 19th century it made large profits from printing the Bible. Today reference books and dictionaries are its main source of income – although they still print three million Bibles each year.

First dictionary

Dr Samuel Johnson compiled the first English dictionary, published in 1755. He left Oxford University in 1731 without a degree but was later awarded an honorary degree.

The end is not in sight

When work started on the first Oxford English Dictionary in 1879, it was estimated that it would take ten years to complete. After five years, however, the editors had only reached the word 'ant'!

Tons of tome

Today's Oxford English Dictionary runs to 20 volumes containing over half-a-million definitions, weighs in at 68 kilograms (150lbs) and takes up 1.2 metres (4ft) of shelving. Or it is available on CD-ROM.

Humble beginnings

William R. Morris – founder of Oxford's motor industry – started in business at the age of 15 by repairing bicycles from his garden shed in James Street. He opened his first shop at No. 48 High Street in 1901, and later expanded to motorcycle repairs from a shop in Longwall Street.

Morris's motors

William R. Morris (later Viscount Nuffield) launched the Morris Oxford motor car in 1913. The subsequent car assembly plant in Cowley kept the city from the depression of the 1930s that swept the country.

Tucked away tavern
The popular pub called the Turf Tavern, parts of which date back to the 13th century, can only be reached by either of two narrow alleyways.

Marvellous marmalade

Frank Cooper's famous home-made marmalade was first sold from his grocery shop at No. 84 High Street in 1874.

Oxford bags

Oxford bags – wide-legged trousers – became a fashion item in the 1920s. Introduced by Hall's the tailor in the High, it is thought that they were originally designed to be worn over hunting breeches, so the wearer could go straight out to the field from a tutorial.

Oldest coffee house

Queen's Lane Coffee House stands at No. 40 High Street. It was from this site in 1654 that Cirques Jobson first sold the new drink known as coffee, making this the oldest coffee house in Europe.

The Old Sheep Shop

The Old Sheep Shop (now Alice's Shop) referred to in Lewis Carroll's *Through the Looking-Glass* is where Alice used to buy barley sugar. The shopkeeper had a bleating voice, so Carroll made her into a sheep in the story.

Blackwell's

Blackwell's is one of the world's largest bookshops and occupies most of the buildings in Broad Street, but when it opened in 1879 to sell second-hand books it was so small that it could only admit three customers at a time.

Four forks

The name Carfax (Oxford's busy crossroads) takes its name from the Latin *quadrifurcus* which means 'four forks'.

Up and down for town and gown

Carfax Tower was made taller in the 14th century, but lowered when the university complained about missiles being thrown from it during clashes between town and gown.

Martyrs' cross

Broad Street was originally the site of a deep ditch outside the city wall where the Oxford Martyrs were burned at the stake in the 16th century. A simple cross in the street-paving marks the spot.

Street lighting

The lamp standards in Merton Street were lit by gas until the 1970s.

Twirl or Turl?

Turl Street gets its names from the 'twirl gate' (turnstile) that once stood in the city wall.

Ghostly happenings III

New College Lane, where Royalist forces gathered before battle during the English Civil War, is said to echo with the sound of ghostly horses' hooves.

Halley's comet
Edmund Halley, the 18th-century astronomer, discovered the comet that bears his name from the observatory at his home in New College Lane.

Royal birthplace

Beaumont Street is built on the site of Beaumont Palace, the birthplace of Richard I.

Through the rabbit hole

At the end of Beaumont Street is a tunnel leading to a lovely garden, the image used by Lewis Carroll when Alice tumbled down the rabbit hole in *Alice's Adventures in Wonderland*.

When Harry met Alice

In 2002, to promote Oxford's links with children's literature, Harry Potter was welcomed at Oxford station by Alice in Wonderland, complete with tray of jam tarts. Over 100 people – including Harry – had travelled on the *Orient Express*, pulled by the *Flying Scotsman* to recreate the billowing steam of *Hogwarts Express*.

First physic garden

The Botanic Garden was the first physic garden in Britain, founded in 1621 by the Earl of Danby as a university faculty for the growing of plants and herbs for medicinal research. It was originally known as the Oxford Physick Garden and was started with the aid of '4,000 loads of mucke and dunge'.

Running amok

In the 19th century the yellow-flowered Oxford Ragwort, originally brought from Mount Etna, escaped from the Botanic Garden and quickly spread all over the country.

First balloon flight

In 1784 James Sadler made the first hot-air balloon flight in Britain from Oxford's Botanic Garden.

Oldest and largest

Port Meadow, mentioned in the Domesday Book, is England's oldest and largest meadow at 160 hectares (400 acres).

Round 'em up

Once a year the Sheriff of Oxford rounds up the animals grazing on Port Meadow and fines any owners who are using the land illegally.

St Giles' Fair

The earliest record of St Giles' Fair, still held each September, dates from 1624. Originally a religious festival, in Victorian times it became popular for its freak shows and female wrestlers.

Between the rivers

The walk known as Mesopotamia between
two parts of the River Cherwell is named
from the Greek for 'between the rivers'.

Oxford Canal

I have observed great storms and
   trembled: I have wept for fear of the dark.
But nothing makes me so afraid as the
   clear water of this idle canal on a
   summer's noon.

From 'Oxford Canal'
   by James Elroy
    (Herman) Flecker
     (1884–1915),
    who attended
   Trinity College

Folly Bridge

Folly Bridge is the site of the original ford where oxen crossed and from which Oxford gets its name.

The Isis

The stretch of the River Thames between Folly Bridge and Iffley Lock is known locally as the Isis.

Iffley Lock

'We passed through Iffley lock at about half past twelve, and then, having tidied up the boat and made all ready for landing, we set to work on our last mile.'

Jerome K. Jerome,
Three Men in a Boat, 1889

Revealing all

Until recently it was usual, when punting, for women to alight and walk round the part of the river known as Parson's Pleasure, which was reserved for nude bathing by male academics.

Father William

Eel traps on a backwater of the Thames at Godstow are reputed to be the inspiration for a verse in Lewis Carroll's poem 'Father William':

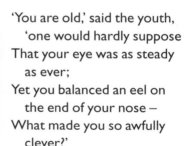

'You are old,' said the youth,
'one would hardly suppose
That your eye was as steady
as ever;
Yet you balanced an eel on
the end of your nose –
What made you so awfully
clever?'

Torpids and Eights Week

Torpids and Eights Week are the names
for the university's two major rowing
events, held in the spring and summer
terms respectively.

Head of the River

The largest pub in Oxford is the Head of

the River, named
after the rowing
event where the
boats start one
behind the other
and each crew
attempts to
catch up with and
bump the boat in
front. The
winning team is
said to be 'Head
of the River'.

Anyone for cricket?

Cricketing legends Colin Cowdrey and Imran Khan are both products of the Oxford University Cricket Club.

Four-minute mile

At a meet in Oxford on 6 May 1954, Roger Bannister was the first person to run a mile (1.6 kilometres) in less than 4 minutes, breaking the barrier at 3 minutes 59.4 seconds.

OUFC

Oxford United Football Club started as a village team in 1893.

Boat race

The Oxford v. Cambridge University Boat Race was first rowed in 1829. Oxford won.

Growing old, growing young

'Oxford changes with every generation. It is always growing old, but it is always growing young again …'.

F. Max Müller,
My Autobiography: a Fragment, 1901